In the Tank

by Andrea Patel
illustrated by Kersti Frigell

Core Decodable 56

Bothell, WA • Chicago, IL • Columbus, OH • New York, NY

MHEonline.com

Copyright © 2015 McGraw-Hill Education

All rights reserved. No part of this publication may be reproduced or distributed in any form or by any means, or stored in a database or retrieval system, without the prior written consent of McGraw-Hill Education, including, but not limited to, network storage or transmission, or broadcast for distance learning.

Send all inquiries to:
McGraw-Hill Education
8787 Orion Place
Columbus, OH 43240

ISBN: 978-0-02-143442-8
MHID: 0-02-143442-5

Printed in the United States of America.

2 3 4 5 6 7 8 9 DOC 20 19 18 17 16 15

Big Bing sits on the tank.
See the pink spot?

I can hit the pink spot.
I can dunk Big Bing.

Big Bing winks.
He thinks I can't dunk him.

Plunk! I hit the pink spot.
Splash! He is in the tank.

I did dunk Big Bing!
He sinks fast.

But he pops up fast.
I think I better run.